Paula Tolbert

D1294550

# Every Kid's Guide to
# Responding
# To Danger

Written by

JOY BERRY

WORD INC.

Waco, TX 76710

## About the Author and Publisher

Joy Berry's mission in life is to help families cope with everyday problems and to help children become competent, responsible, happy individuals. To achieve her goal, she has written over two hundred self-help books for children from infancy through age twelve. Her work has revolutionized children's publishing by providing families with practical, how-to, living skills information that was previously unavailable in children's books.

Joy has gathered a dedicated team of experts, including psychologists, educators, child developmentalists, writers, editors, designers, and artists to form her publishing company and to help produce her work.

The company, Living Skills Press, produces thoroughly researched books and audiovisual materials that successfully combine humor and education to teach children subjects ranging from how to clean a bedroom to how to resolve problems and get along with other people.

Managing Editor: Ellen Klarberg
Copy Editor: Annette Gooch
Contributing Editors: Libby Byers, Nancy Cochran, Maureen Dryden,
Yoná Flemming, Kathleen Mohr, Susan Motycka
Editorial Assistant: Lana Eberhard

Art Director: Jennifer Wiezel
Designers: Laurie Westdahl, Jennifer Wiezel
Production Artists: Susie Hornig, Jennifer Wiezel

Typographer: Communication Graphics

Illustrations created in cooperation with Comm-Spot
Design: Bartholomew
Art Direction: Ronald J. Garnier, Thomas Karleskint
Inking: Nancy Strothkamp, Dave Moore
Coloring: Susan Launis, Fran Ray

0-8499-8602-8
890123 RRD 987654321

There are dangers all around you. In **Every Kid's Guide To Responding To Danger,** you will learn about

- ■ fear,
- ■ dangerous objects,
- ■ using dangerous objects appropriately,
- ■ dangerous places,
- ■ responding to dangerous places appropriately,
- ■ dangerous situations, and
- ■ responding to dangerous situations appropriately.

A *danger* is something that can injure or harm you.

One of your best protections against danger is *fear.*
Your fear often tells you when danger is near.

It is important to pay attention to your fear and respond to it appropriately.

One appropriate response to your fear is to **avoid whatever is causing you to be afraid.**

Another appropriate response to your fear is to **be careful around whatever is causing you to be afraid.**

Paying attention to your fear and responding to it appropriately can help you handle the dangers around you.

The dangers around you include
- **dangerous objects,**
- **dangerous places, and**
- **dangerous situations.**

Objects that can harm you or someone else are dangerous.

**_Aerosol and spray cans_** can be dangerous if they are not used properly. The contents of an aerosol or spray can might harm you if sprayed in your eyes, nose, or mouth. Also, aerosol cans might explode and injure you if they become too hot.

***Chemicals,*** such as medicines and cleaning products, can be dangerous if they are not used properly. Chemicals can make you very sick and even kill you if you swallow or inhale them. Also, touching some chemicals can damage your skin.

***Kitchen utensils,*** such as knives, can be dangerous. Utensils can cut you if they are not used properly.

*Razors* can be dangerous. Razors can scrape or cut you if they are not used properly.

***Recreational equipment,*** such as slingshots, darts, and archery sets, can be dangerous. These objects can injure your body or cause blindness if they are not used properly.

*Guns* can be dangerous if they are not used properly. A bullet shot from a gun can injure your body or kill you.

*Electrical appliances* can be dangerous if they are not used properly. You can get an electrical shock if you are wet or standing in water when you plug in an appliance.

You can also get a shock by putting something other than an electrical plug into an electrical outlet. Electrical shocks can kill you.

*Hand tools,* such as axes, hammers, saws, and screwdrivers, can be dangerous.

*Power tools,* such as electric drills, saws, and sanders, can also be dangerous.

All of these objects can injure you or kill you if they are not used properly.

*Fire* can be dangerous. Fire can damage or destroy things if it is not used properly. Fire can also injure or kill people.

*Explosives,* such as firecrackers, can be dangerous if they are not used properly. They can cause you to become blind or deaf if they explode too close to your eyes or ears. They can also cause burns or other serious injuries.

The following rules will help you use objects properly:

**Rule 1. Be sure you know everything you need to know about the objects you use.**

Ask your parents or guardians to help you decide whether or not you know enough about an object to use it.

**Rule 2. Be sure you are strong enough to handle the objects you use.**

Ask your parents or guardians to help you decide whether or not you have enough strength to use something.

**Rule 3. Learn to use the objects correctly.**

**Rule 4. Use objects the way that they are meant to be used.**

**Rule 5. Do not abuse the objects you use.**

Rule 6. Make sure an adult is nearby and knows what you are doing whenever you use an object that could be dangerous.

Places where you or someone else could get hurt are dangerous.

*Animal enclosures,* such as cages, corrals, and fenced-in areas, can be dangerous. If you go into these enclosures, the animals inside them might hurt you.

*Animal trails* can be dangerous. If you get in the way of animals using them, you might be hurt.

***Driveways and parking lots*** can be dangerous. A vehicle that has stopped can begin to move and might hit you.

**Streets and highways** can be dangerous. If you get in the path of a moving vehicle, it might hit you.

*Enclosed spaces,* such as closets, refrigerators, and freezers, can be dangerous. They do not contain very much air. If you get inside one of these enclosed spaces and do not have enough air to breathe, you might die.

*Places where large machines are located* can be dangerous. If you get too close to the machines, you might be injured or even killed.

*High places* can be dangerous. If you fall off them, you might get hurt.

*Big holes in the ground* can be dangerous. If you fall into one, it can be difficult or even impossible for you to get out of it.

*Large bodies of water,* such as pools, lakes, ponds, and rivers, can be dangerous. If you cannot swim or if you are not careful, you might drown in them.

*Polluted areas,* where there are a lot of fumes, smoke, dirt, and grime in the air and on the ground, can be dangerous. Being around these areas too long can make you very sick.

*Caves* can be dangerous. You cannot see clearly in a cave. This makes it difficult to avoid the dangers that can be inside.

*Unexplored or uninhabited areas* can be dangerous. When you do not know an area, you do not know what to avoid. You might experience a danger that you cannot handle.

If you are like most people, you might be curious about a dangerous area. You might want to explore it. If you want to explore a dangerous area, there are four steps you need to follow:

**Step 1. Ask an adult to go with you.**

## Step 2. Carefully inspect the dangerous area with the adult.

### Step 3. Talk with the adult about the dangerous area.

Share your thoughts and feelings about the place. Ask any questions you might have. Listen carefully to what the adult has to say about the area.

**Step 4. Promise that you will not go near the place again unless an adult is with you or the place is made safe.**

Then keep your promise.

Dangerous situations are events that can hurt you.

*Natural disasters,* such as earthquakes, tornadoes, hurricanes, and floods, are dangerous situations.

**Disasters caused by people,** such as fires, accidents, and explosions, are dangerous situations.

*Criminal acts,* such as robbery and kidnapping, are dangerous situations.

*Encounters with wild, mean, or unfamiliar animals* can create dangerous situations.

If you are like most people, you do not want to experience dangerous situations. To avoid dangerous situations, you need to learn as much as you can about them. If you know about dangerous situations, you will most likely know how to avoid them.

Sometimes no matter what you do, you cannot avoid a dangerous situation. When this happens, it is good to know how to respond to it in the right way. To learn how to handle dangerous situations, you can

- talk to people,
- watch appropriate programs on TV, and
- read books, magazines, and newspapers .

The dangers that surround you will not harm you if you avoid them or handle them properly.